A Sister in White

The Story of Schvester Selma

Great Women, Great Stories
Biographies of Notable Jewish Women

A Sister in White
The Story of Schvester Selma

Miriam Zakon

TARGUM/FELDHEIM

Phototypeset at Targum Press

Published by:
Targum Press Inc.
22700 W. Eleven Mile Rd.
Southfield, Mich. 48034

Distributed by:
Feldheim Publishers
200 Airport Executive Park
Nanuet, N.Y. 10954

Distributed in Israel by:
Targum Press Ltd.
POB 43170
Jerusalem 91430

Printed in Israel

Great Women, Great Stories is sponsored by Keren Etz HaTamar,
POB 34329, Jerusalem 91342.

A Note to My Readers

This book is about a very unusual woman who lived in a very unusual time. In the very unusual city of Jerusalem. Her name was Selma Meir.

She lived for a hundred years and accomplished a lot. Though she was famous in the city in which she lived, few people outside of Jerusalem have ever heard of Selma Meir. That's a shame, because her life was both interesting and inspiring. Her story is worth reading. So here it is.

All the main characters you will meet in these pages really lived. All the stories you will read in this book really did happen — even the ones that sound unbelievable. I heard them all from people who were there at the time.

Some thank you's:

A lot of wonderful people helped me get the information about Schvester Selma and the times she lived in. Leah Abramowitz sent me to some very interesting women who had learned from Schvester Selma and worked with her. Tzila Perele, Miriam Falk, and Margit Lehman were all Shaare Zedek nurses, and each of them spent a lot of time telling me fascinating stories (and giving me cups of tea and generous pieces of delicious homemade cake!). I loved meeting them and thank them for their time.

In Shaare Zedek, Uri Schwarz and Dvora Wilschansky gave me good advice. Sharon Alter got the photographs together for me. Yisrael Nir, a fascinating man who volunteers in Shaare Zedek and is translating their old documents from German into Hebrew, read the manuscript and told me some very interesting things. All together, the Shaare Zedek public-relations team have been very helpful and nice to work with.

A Sister in White is the first in what we hope will be a series of books on great Jewish women. Do you want to discuss Schvester Selma's life with me? Or do you have any ideas for other biographies? You can contact me at targum@elronet.co.il. I look forward to hearing from you.

Miriam Zakon

Shvester Selma, as she will always be remembered

Selma as a young woman

Chapter 1
Taking the Test

Germany, 1913

The professor at the front of the classroom looked very fierce. He had a black mustache. His beard was so stiff that it seemed almost to be carved out of black marble. He sat absolutely upright in his uncomfortable-looking high-backed chair. Before him sat thirty young ladies, looking almost as stiff as the professor. They were all dressed in white. Their long white skirts were so heavily starched they rustled when the girls moved. Each had a clean white apron tied neatly around her waist. Their white collars were as hard as cardboard. The collars were not very pleasant to wear around their necks, but the girls hardly noticed their discomfort. They were concentrating too hard on the pile of papers before them.

The professor's stern glance fell upon a student sitting in the second row. She was very short, tinier than any of the other girls. Yet something about her caught his eye. Perhaps it was the way she sat so straight in her chair. Maybe it was the confident way in which she dipped her pen in her inkwell. He noticed that her white blouse glowed and sparkled even among the sea of white uniforms surrounding her. Or maybe it was the glow and sparkle of her eyes that caught his attention. Those blue eyes looked out on the world with a mixture of caring and laughter and understanding. *This one*, thought the professor to himself, without moving a muscle in his face, *this one is a true nurse*.

The girl in the second row, unaware of the professor's gaze, continued to write in her answers. This was the final test she was to take. She was hoping to be awarded a diploma that would make her an official, licensed nurse in Germany. It was a difficult challenge. The professors didn't make it easy to pass. In addition to completing a tough written test, each of the young women had to prove she could deal with the practical part of nursing. They had to make beds, bathe patients, prepare instruments for the doctors, change bloody bandages, and diaper newborn babies.

The girl in the second row had done all this and more. For seven years, she'd been working as a nurse in the Salomon Heine Hospital in Hamburg, Germany. Now, for the first time, Jewish nurses were being allowed to actually take the tests for the German State Diploma. Tiny Selma Meir, sitting and diligently writing in the second row, was determined to pass.

The weeks went by. Selma impatiently waited to hear how she had done. When the results came in, Selma found she'd done more than pass the test. She and another Jewish woman had received top marks. Even the fierce professor seemed proud of her accomplishment. As he handed her her diploma, his stiff mustache seemed to relax a little into the ghost of a smile.

In Germany, nurses are known by the honorable title of *schvester*, which means "sister." So it was on that day in 1913, in the German city of Hamburg, that Selma Meir became Schvester Selma. It was a title she would wear proudly for more than seventy years.

Carriage, camel, and donkey bring the sick to Shaare Zedek Hospital in Jerusalem

Chapter 2
Trains and Donkeys

Europe, 1916

The train slowly puffed and smoked its way up the mountain. Selma Meir stared out the tiny window. She tried to ignore the soot and grime that lay thickly on the glass. Up, up the train climbed, leaving tiny villages and strange rock formations behind.

The thin ribbon of train track seemed to wind through the mountains all the way up to the cloudy gray sky. *Perhaps it will reach clear up to heaven*, Selma thought, laughing to herself.

Suddenly, as the train rounded a curve, Selma saw a giant wall of dark rock. Were they going to crash right into the mountainside?

They grew closer to the sharp and forbidding mountain that lay before them. Then, with a sigh of relief,

Selma noticed a tiny split in the wall of harsh rock. It was a mountain pass so narrow that the train could barely fit through it. The train chugged on, its whistle echoing eerily off the high walls on either side.

The train screeched to a halt not long after they'd roared through the mountain pass. A young soldier appeared in the smoky car. He was wearing a brown uniform with shiny gold buttons. He had a brown turban on his head. The bullets hanging on his chest gave him a sinister and frightening look. "Papers! Prepare your papers!" he shouted.

The soldier, whose name was Mustapha, made his way up and down the aisle. He stopped at every passenger's side and carefully checked each one's travel papers. Mustapha took his job seriously. After all, his country, Turkey, was fighting the Great War against the Allies. Spies were everywhere, and he, Mustapha, was determined to find them!

He paused next to a short, dark-haired woman. "Papers!" he barked.

The woman opened a brown leather case. "Here they are," she said quietly. She quickly handed him a pile of documents. Many of the papers bore the official stamp of the Turkish empire.

Something in her voice made Mustapha look up. The woman spoke in German. German is usually a harsh language, but coming from her it sounded pleasant to his ears, almost like music.

Pulling his attention back to the documents, he read

through them. He carefully noted her name. "You are Selma Meir, traveling from Frankfurt to Palestine via Syria?"

The woman gave him a nod and a brief smile. Again, Mustapha was struck by something in her face. She was not frightened of him, of his uniform and loud voice, as were some of the passengers. She was not bored by the endless questions as she passed from one country to the other. No, this woman was...kind. He could see that in her eyes.

The soldier passed on to the next seat. Selma turned to a dignified man sitting beside her. "I almost handed him the wrong travel papers, Dr. Auerbach," she said with a smile. "So many documents, so many countries!"

"Did you imagine it would be such a difficult journey?" Dr. Auerbach asked her.

Selma's mind went back over the past few busy weeks. She remembered the head nurse in Salomon Heine Hospital calling her into the small supply room that served as an office.

"Schvester Selma," she had said in that curt way she had of speaking, "you are aware that you have been chosen to be part of our war service."

Selma met her gaze and nodded. The year 1916, and her country, Germany, was in the midst of a brutal and drawn-out war against England, France, and their allies. As a trained nurse, Schvester Selma Meir was expected to do her part in the war effort.

"A doctor has been to see me. Dr. Wallach is his

name. Some years ago he opened a hospital in Palestine. In Jerusalem."

Selma's thin dark eyebrows shot up slightly. Palestine?

"Dr. Wallach is looking for a head nurse for his hospital. I believe you would suit him, and you would be allowed to do your war service there. Would you care to go?"

Would she care to go? Selma Meir was never one to show her emotions openly. But though her face remained cool and calm, her thoughts were swift and frenzied.

Palestine? As a Jew, Selma had, of course, heard of that backward, primitive country in the Middle East. Palestine, after all, was simply another name for Eretz Yisrael, the Land of Israel. Palestine was a Jewish dream, a Jewish hope for two thousand years. But to live there? In a tiny, remote, almost-forgotten corner that belonged to Germany's allies, the Turks? To leave her home in Germany? Germany was civilized and artistic. Here she fit in so well.

While her thoughts bubbled and brewed like the potatoes being cooked in the hospital's kitchen, the head nurse had continued to speak. Her words suddenly caught Selma's wandering attention.

"The hospital was originally built with forty beds, but the demand is much greater. There are many outbreaks of disease. The care of the orphans is shocking. But Dr. Wallach says that..."

Orphans. Selma swallowed hard. She knew little

about Middle-Eastern politics and less about the Ottoman Empire, but she knew all about orphans. Selma's mother had died when she, Selma, had been very young, little more than a baby. Her family had taken care of little Selma, but all her life she'd missed the sweetness of a mother's love. When Selma had seen other youngsters happily sitting on a mother's lap or enjoying a mother's hug, she hadn't grown bitter or jealous. Instead, she became determined to give to others that which she had never had: love.

The thought of those orphans in that desert country overcame all doubts. Hardly knowing what she was doing, Schvester Selma agreed to sign a contract. For the next three years she would take on the job of head nurse in Dr. Wallach's hospital in Jerusalem.

The weeks that followed passed in a haze of travel papers, packing, and farewells. There was so much to do! With the world at war, it was decided that a young lady should not travel by herself. Dr. Moses Auerbach, a prominent educator who lived in Jerusalem, was traveling through Germany at the time. At Dr. Wallach's request, he agreed to accompany the new head nurse. Selma had spent many hours of her train ride speaking with him, learning much about the city she was to come help nurse. The rest of the seemingly endless journey she spent in a dream, wondering what awaited her at her final destination.

The trip from Germany to Palestine was a long one. It took the traveler through three empires and seven countries. From Berlin to Budapest, then on to the Balkan Express that chugged through Rumania and Bulgaria. On and on they traveled, at last coming to a stop in the train station of the Turkish capital, Constantinople. From there the weary travelers boarded still another train to take them through the Taurus and Amanus mountain ranges in Anatolia. Over the border into Syria, where they waited three days for the train that would take them to Jerusalem.

Finally, the journey came to an end. The steam whistle gave a shrill cry as the bright blue and red engine pulled into its final destination, Jerusalem. Dr. Auerbach politely held the metal door open as Selma, dusty, tired, but still smiling, carefully stepped down onto the soil of Palestine.

It was noisy and confusing in the train station. Men wearing strange-looking checkered headdresses sold odd-smelling spices. Beggars with horrendous open sores whined for a coin or two. Skinny cats and skinnier children walked lightly and aimlessly through the large terminal. Porters hauled luggage onto overloaded carts.

A swarthy old man approached the young nurse, who stood gazing at the tumult before her. His shoulders stooped beneath years of carrying others' burdens. He gave her a smile, revealing two missing front teeth.

"Wallach? Wallach?" he growled.

"I'm Selma Meir. Has Dr. Wallach sent you to meet me?"

The man gave her a delighted grin and grabbed her

bulky valise. He lifted her heavy packages easily despite his age. He set down the luggage onto a battered cart and motioned to his passenger to climb up next to him. Selma pulled herself up onto the hard wooden bench. She gave the white donkey hitched onto the cart a wary look and pulled her shawl closer around her. She felt glad for the fur around her collar and her elegant black gloves. They would keep her warm in the frosty night air. She gave Dr. Auerbach a final farewell wave and sat back, her eyes sparkling. Her adventure had begun!

The cart clip-clopped through rocky, barren terrain. Finally, they reached a wall carved out of huge rocks. A great clock tower peeked out over the wall. Its bells chimed the hour: eight o'clock. Again, as in the train station, there was a great confusion of noise. Beggars and children milled around the arched gateway. Selma noticed Arabic letters carved over the lintel. She wondered what they meant.

The donkey plodded through the gate and halted in front of a two-story building. "Hotel Amdursky," a sign proclaimed.

Selma jumped off the cart. She felt mud splash on her traveling suit. As she turned toward the hotel's ornately carved wooden door, a dark-clad figure walked out of it.

"Schvester Selma? I am Dr. Wallach. Welcome to Jerusalem."

Dr. Moshe Wallach, first director of Shaare Zedek

Chapter 3

Jerusalem of Old

Jerusalem, 1916

When you're short, less than five feet tall, you get used to bending your neck back to look people in the eye. As Selma gazed at the figure standing before her, she realized that *Herr Doktor* was not much taller than she was. She saw a stocky figure, very square: square shoulders, square white beard, square black silk yarmulke on his head. So this was Dr. Wallach, the man who had somehow gotten her to travel to this dusty and forgotten corner of the world.

During their train trip together, Dr. Auerbach had told her a little about the man who was to be her superior in the hospital. Like Selma, Dr. Wallach, too, had come to Palestine from Germany. He'd left his hometown of Cologne more than thirty years before, in the

late 1800s. Before this, the only hospitals in the city that
could perform operations and take care of very sick patients were run by Christian groups. Unfortunately, they
often tried to persuade their Jewish patients to convert.
For this reason, most Jews stayed far away — and often
died for lack of medical care.

Jerusalem's rabbis turned to Germany for help, and
soon a committee of German Jews, headed by the famous Rabbi Shamshon Rafael Hirsch, was formed. In
1893, the committee hired Dr. Moshe Wallach, who was
only twenty-six years old, and sent him to Jerusalem.

Dr. Wallach was a very religious man and a very
good doctor. In a short time, many of the residents of the
city — Jews and non-Jews alike — came to rely on him.
In 1902 Dr. Wallach realized his dream when he opened
a forty-bed hospital. Because the Turks didn't want to
sell him land in Jerusalem's Old City, where most of the
people lived, this became the first new Jewish hospital to
be built outside the Old City walls. The hospital's official name was Shaare Zedek. But city residents knew
better: they all called it Wallach's Hospital.

Though Dr. Auerbach had spoken of Dr. Wallach's
history and accomplishments, of his character he had
said nothing. That would remain for Schvester Selma to
find out.

"Welcome to Jerusalem," Dr. Wallach repeated. His
voice was gravelly. It was almost a bark and yet, somehow, not unkind. "You must be tired after your journey.
Come in and refresh yourself."

As she sat down gratefully in the hotel's small and musty parlor, Selma spoke for the first time.

"I would be grateful for a hot cup of coffee. With milk."

"Milk?" Dr. Wallach shot her a piercing glance. His eyes wandered toward a large grandfather clock standing in a corner of the room. "It's not long after dinner. Are you certain that you haven't supped on meat in the past few hours?"

Though surprised by his bluntness, Selma gave him a thin smile. "Dr. Wallach, I have just completed a four-week journey. In that entire month, I can tell you I haven't even seen a piece of meat!"

Dr. Wallach laughed. Strange how his entire body seemed to change when he did. It was as if some light had gone on inside of him, glowing within his deep eyes.

He barked a few words in Arabic at the waiter hovering around them. The waiter disappeared. He returned a few minutes later holding a bronze tray with a small white cup on it. Inside, Selma could see a muddy-looking liquid. It smelled strange, though not unattractive. *This wasn't the kind of coffee they drank in Germany*, she thought, as she cautiously gave a sip. Outside, she could hear some kind of Arabic chant. Yes, Germany and home were certainly far away!

"And now," Dr. Wallach said, "you can either stay here and rest up from your journey" — his eyes gazed thoughtfully at the slight figure lying back in a deep upholstered chair — "or you can accompany me back to the hospital."

Selma hesitated. The chair was comfortable. The journey had, indeed, been long and tiring. How nice it would be to stay here. She would love to enjoy the privacy of her own room. It would be wonderful to climb into a clean bed with a hot-water bottle tucked between snow-white sheets to keep her warm.

She stretched herself up to her full height. "I've come here to work, not to rest," she said briskly. "I'll go back with you."

Dr. Wallach gave a slight approving nod, then jumped out of his seat to arrange transportation.

Oh, well, Selma thought, as she watched her trunks being hauled back onto another donkey cart, *the bed in the hospital will also be there for me.*

Snow-white sheets? A hot-water bottle? A clean bed? *What have I gotten myself into?* Selma thought as she looked around the large, dimly lit room.

The nursing staff, Dr. Wallach had explained as he led Selma down a pair of dark stone steps, slept in the basement.

Selma felt anger well up within her. She'd been promised a private room of her own! She clamped her lips tightly together, determined not to begin her job here with a complaint. Still, the injustice of it bothered her.

Dr. Wallach continued to speak. "We've had to move the nurses out of their own quarters to make room

The hospital in the early 1900s

for more patients. We've got 150 patients right now."

"One hundred and fifty? But I was told this was a forty-bed hospital."

"It is. But not when we're in the midst of an epidemic."

"Epidemic?" Selma felt her heart beat faster.

"That's right. Typhoid. So you see, you couldn't have come at a better time, Schvester Selma."

A better time is rather a strange way to describe it, Selma thought. But she soon began to understand what Dr. Wallach meant as he painted a picture of the city she was to call home for the next three years.

"The dirt, the disease, is terrible," the doctor told her gravely. "It's not the people's fault. Water is always in short supply. Rainwater is kept in stone cisterns and used year round. There's not enough to wash properly. The housing shortage is unbelievable. We have entire families living in one room. Six, eight children sleep on mattresses, one on top of the other. Epidemics, diseases that are passed from person to person, are common. Sometimes it's malaria, keeping patients shivering all night with fever. Sometimes it's diphtheria, with its horrible, wracking cough. Now, we face the most dreaded killer of all, typhoid fever."

"But can't something be done about the dirt and the living conditions?" Selma asked. She was horrified at what she was hearing.

"Done? This is wartime, Schvester Selma. Not enough food, not enough medicines. And our esteemed overlords, the Turks, at the best of times have not been very generous to our people."

Dr. Wallach looked down at his large pocket watch. He could barely see it in the room's dusty dimness. "Time for my rounds. I'll expect you to join me tomorrow morning. At seven sharp." His voice softened somewhat. "Get a good night's sleep, Schvester. There's a lot of work to be done."

Selma stared at the two large trunks the porter had dropped by her feet. Ignoring her aching muscles, she carefully opened one of them. She pulled out several sweaters one at a time, gave each a shake and folded it neatly, laying one on top of the other on the only flat space she could find, her own bed. Then she turned to put them into the wooden closet next to the bed. She opened the doors and gasped slightly. The shelves were crammed with hospital linens! One small shelf had been cleaned off for the personal use of the hospital's new *schvester*.

Selma rolled her eyes. With a sigh she swept the sweaters off her bed and put them back into her trunk. They would stay there for close to a year, until the brutal typhoid epidemic had finally come under control and the nurse from Germany could get the private room she'd been promised.

That night Selma lay in bed, her eyes open. She was so tired she felt weighed down with heavy ropes. Still, she was unable to sleep. The images of the past few hours danced before her eyes. She saw Dr. Wallach, with his dark coat, white beard, and stern face. She remembered the porter, the muscles on his thin arms like taut iron chains. She could still feel the donkey cart jolting up and down unpaved muddy streets. She could almost hear the peddlers and the beggars and the children with their filthy faces and red, runny eyes. She remembered snatches of conversation, dread words. Epidemic. One hundred and fifty patients for forty beds. "Get a good night's sleep, Schvester. There's a lot of work to be done."

Morning came to Jerusalem. Thin rays of sunshine managed to make their way into the basement room. They snuck in through cracks in the green shutters that covered the few small windows overlooking the hospital's garden. Once inside, the rays seemed to dance upon the dust motes floating in the air. Finally, they came to rest upon a sleeping face. The rest of the workers using the basement, mostly poor women employed in the kitchen and as cleaning help, had been up way before sunrise. Only Schvester Selma lay still, ready to be tickled into wakefulness by the mischievous sunshine.

But it wasn't the sunshine that broke Schvester Selma's deep sleep. It was the sound of someone shouting.

"No! No! Absolutely not! Haven't I told you a thousand times not to hold a baby like that?"

The figure on the uncomfortable, pallet-like mattress stirred, stretched, and then shot upright. What in the world was that undignified noise coming from the hospital ward above her? What kind of hospital was this anyway?

She glanced at the window. Sunshine! Had she overslept on this, her first day here? Selma grabbed the modest watch she kept with her always. She looked at the dust-covered window not far from her bed and pulled the shutters open. Seconds later, she slammed them shut with a muffled shriek. What was that thing out there? Slowly, willing her heart to stop pounding, Selma carefully opened the shutter once again, this time just a crack. Then she burst into laughter. A camel's mild, slightly stupid face poked into the window with incurious, patient eyes.

I certainly am far away from home, Selma thought as she gazed back at the creature. Putting this thought — and the stab of homesickness that shot through her — carefully in the back of her mind, she once again picked up the watch. She was in luck — only six-thirty. Something else to get used to: sunrise in this strange, tropical land came earlier here than in her home country.

It didn't take her long to dress, particularly since the only washing water that seemed to be available was lukewarm, left in a small, cracked ewer next to her bed. A person wasn't disposed to linger in the coolness of the room's stone walls anyway. Selma looked around for a fireplace and saw none, only a small kerosene heater that sat, quiet and forlorn, in a corner. As she dressed, she heard repeated shouts coming from above. *This isn't a hospital; it's more like a zoo,* she thought, *with all the noise going on above me.*

At ten minutes to seven, her skirt and apron starched, white, and immaculate, she walked up the stairs, ready to face the new day — camels and shouting and all.

Making the rounds — Dr. Wallach and Schvester Selma

Chapter 4

The New Schvester

Jerusalem, 1916

For the first two weeks in Jerusalem, Selma became the doctor's white-clad shadow. She went from bed to bed, from ward to ward, a pad in her hand. Patients saw a short, quiet woman with kind eyes. What they didn't see was the despair and shock that gripped her heart as she realized just what she'd taken on in this new assignment.

As Dr. Wallach had told her, Schvester Selma had arrived at the height of a terrible epidemic. On one of her first days in Jerusalem, Selma, feeling almost dizzy from the fumes of the kerosene heaters, stepped out for a little winter sunshine. Leaving the hospital grounds to take a walk on Jaffa Road, she tread her way carefully. She'd already lost one pair of boots in the thick, unyielding mud of the unpaved street! Selma walked out the

Patients coming for treatment

door and noticed a crowd of people lined up noisily in front of the building. Some were pushing. Others, too tired to shove, had plopped down wearily right onto the muddy ground. Mothers, their faces pale with worry, held crying babies in their arms. Old men leaned on sticks or on the arms of their children.

Selma approached a woman wearing a ragged black dress, far too thin for the winter's chill. She asked what the crowd wanted. The woman stared, but she didn't understand Selma's crisp German. A man standing next to her answered in accented Yiddish, "We're waiting to get into Wallach's Hospital."

"But why?" Selma was puzzled.

"Sick. All of us, sick. We need Dr. Wallach to help us."

Selma's gaze ran over the long, curving line of suffering people. She gasped. The mob reached back, back, as far as the city's *shuk*, its market, over five blocks away!

All these people needed help. All these people needed Dr. Wallach. All these people needed her.

She rushed back into the hospital to continue her work.

So this was the state of the city she was to call home for the next three years. Three years! And the state of the hospital she'd joined was even worse. For nursing staff she had several untrained young girls and one jolly Persian who smelled of garlic. There had been a few trained nurses from Germany, Dr. Wallach told her. "But they couldn't bear the conditions here," he said grimly.

I will bear the conditions here, Selma thought to herself. *And I will create a wonderful hospital.*

After two weeks spent seeing all that was to be seen, Schvester Selma was ready to start on the difficult task she had chosen for herself. She called together all the hospital workers. They had already met their new head nurse. They thought she was a pleasant little lady. A bit quiet. Not at all like Dr. Wallach, who was always shouting at them. Not what one would call a powerful woman, it seemed.

It seemed that they were wrong.

"First of all," she said, "let me congratulate you on the job you've done until now. You've worked very hard, under terribly difficult conditions."

The workers nodded at each other. They were pleased to hear this. Dr. Wallach always demanded perfection and always found things they'd done wrong. Here was a woman who appreciated them!

"I have come from Germany and there have learned some new things that we will be putting into place here."

The workers exchanged glances. Changes? They didn't like the sound of this.

"I have ordered white clothing for all of you. They will arrive next week. You will wear them."

Dudu was a large, brown-skinned woman with flashing eyes who worked in the hospital's laundry room. She hooted with laughter. "What's wrong with our clothing, may I ask, madam?"

Schvester Selma spoke quietly. "I am not 'madam.' I am Schvester Selma. The head nurse in this hospital."

"So, Schvester," Dudu laughed again, "I repeat, what's wrong with our clothing?"

"There is nothing wrong with your clothing. They are fine — for when you are in your homes. In a hospital, all workers wear white. This hospital will be kept clean and professional. That includes white uniforms."

Schvester Selma continued her crisp lecture. "Patients will be washed every day. Those who can bathe will do so themselves. Those who cannot will be bathed by our workers."

Tzipa, a young girl training to be a nurse, looked at Schvester Selma, shocked. "Bathed every day? In the winter? They will die of cold!"

Schvester Selma gave the girl a kind look. "No, they will not die of cold. They will be bathed and dried, and they will grow strong and healthy and clean."

On and on it went. Schvester Selma, the quiet little

head nurse, demanded even more of the workers than Dr. Wallach did. She wanted the hospital to be kept clean. Slowly, they learned to keep it clean. She wanted every patient to be treated well, even the very poor, even the very nasty. They learned to treat everyone well, no matter who he or she was.

One Tuesday morning, Schvester Selma again called together the hospital workers. "When a patient comes in with a contagious disease such as typhoid, he or she must be bathed immediately. Whoever does so must wear special clothing, which will then be sent to be washed in boiling hot water."

"More washing! She's going to kill us, this new *schvester*," muttered Dudu. But she complained quietly. She had no wish to get into open warfare with Schvester

The laundry room — washing by hand and by early electric washing machine

Selma. But she didn't like it. All these changes meant more and more work.

"It's easy for Schvester Selma to come up with crazy ideas like changing the sheets every day," Dudu said angrily after the head nurse had returned to the ward to check on her patients. "After all, she doesn't have to get her hands red and wrinkled in the hot water!"

"That's not true, Dudu!" Tzippy, the young nurse trainee, stepped up to Schvester Selma's defense. "You know that Schvester Selma works harder than all of us! Nothing is too small for her to do. When it comes to a patient —"

"Patients, yes! I admit that she's like a little mother to the sick," Dudu answered grudgingly. "But clean, clean, clean! It's making me crazy, all this clean!"

"She's got eagle eyes," Tzippy admitted. "Last night I saw her bend down to pick up a pin — a tiny pin — from the floor. Nothing escapes her!"

Suddenly Schvester Selma came in. The two grew silent.

"By the way, Dudu, the towels in the supply cabinet are running low. Do you have more ready for me?"

"More? More?" The washerwoman's dark eyes flashed. "I have no more! They're all gone! Every sick person comes here to get well and thinks he can take home a load of linens as a remembrance of his lovely stay in Wallach's Hospital! You want to know where your towels are? Talk to your beloved patients."

Schvester Selma's eyes twinkled. "Perhaps I will."

Later that day, as Dudu trudged back to the two-room apartment she shared with her husband and five children, she noticed a pair of very straight, white-clad shoulders in front of her. Impossible to mistake that small figure. It was Schvester Selma, walking through the impoverished neighborhood behind the city's vegetable market.

Dudu was intrigued. What did the strange *schvester* from Germany do during her free time? And what was she doing here?

She watched as Schvester Selma walked slowly, her head turned up. She seemed to be staring at something above her. The sky? The birds?

Schvester Selma came to a stop. Immediately above her, a load of white laundry flapped in the winter's breeze.

In the darkness of the building's stairway, it was easy for Dudu to follow Schvester Selma as she walked up to a second-floor apartment. Dudu hung around in the shadowy corners, watching.

Schvester Selma knocked. A pale, tired-looking woman wearing a black kerchief on her head answered the door.

"Hello." Schvester Selma gave her a pleasant smile. "I'm from Dr. Wallach's hospital."

The woman stared at her. She didn't say a word.

"Our hospital is running out of sheets and towels. I happened to notice that you have some of our towels on your line. Do you think I could possibly have them back?"

Dudu watched as the tired woman shyly handed Schvester Selma two white towels. The woman looked as if she was afraid. Perhaps she thought the head nurse would scream at her for having taking hospital property. But Schvester Selma simply smiled, shook her hand warmly, and left.

Again and again Schvester Selma stopped to knock at shabby doors, enter poor apartments, and reclaim hospital towels. Always, behind her, was the shadow of Dudu following her.

The next day, Schvester Selma announced that the nurse's uniforms had to be washed every day. Everyone looked at Dudu, waiting for her to complain. Dudu simply nodded. "It's a good idea, Schvester," she said loudly. "Everyone's got to work to make this a better hospital."

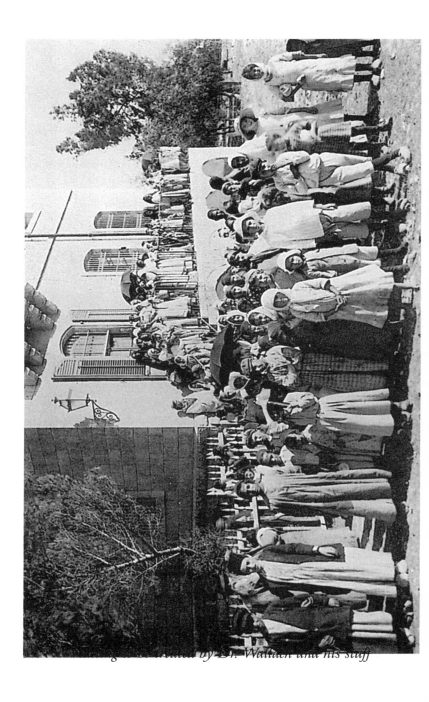

...g ...ted by Dr. Wallach and his staff

Chapter 5

The Incomparable Dr. Wallach

Jerusalem, 1917

H*ave I made a mistake?* Schvester Selma thought as she slowly untied her black bootlaces. *Have I made a mistake in coming to this place?*

Usually, Schvester Selma didn't think these black, unhappy thoughts. She was far too busy for such things. The hospital was still overcrowded, and so many people needed her! She had to teach the young girls working in the wards how to become good nurses. She had to explain to the women in the laundry and the kitchen why it was so important to keep everything clean. And, of course, she had to take care of the patients. She had to feed them, wash them, and change their bandages. She had to make sure the newborn babies were gaining the proper amount of weight. She had to bathe feverish children who cried all through the night. She had to give medicine to old women who hated the bad-tasting syrups and who clamped their mouths shut when the little *schvester* came near them.

On most days Selma simply didn't have the time to complain, but today had been especially difficult. People in Germany had told Selma that Palestine was a tropical, desert country. That meant it was hot. No one had told her that Jerusalem also had winters and that those winters were cold. Very cold. In the past few days the temperature had gone down a lot. The wind had been bitter. Hearing it howl as it came in through the mountains gave Selma the shivers. In Germany it had also been cold, but somehow here the chill got right into the bones and stayed there. In Germany there had been furnaces and fireplaces and goose-down blankets and other ways to keep warm. Here in Jerusalem, if you were lucky you had a small kerosene heater. It would give off a terrible smell and a little — very little — bit of heat.

Cold weather meant more than being uncomfortable. Already, three patients had come in with pneumonia, an infection in the lungs that often came from being chilled. One man, who'd lost his way the night before on the long road between Jaffa and Jerusalem, had actually come in with frostbite on his fingers!

But it wasn't the frigid air in her basement room that made Selma upset. It wasn't even the endless work. It was Dr. Wallach.

Shouting. Always shouting, Schvester Selma thought

to herself. *Yes, he is a good doctor. But he is so strange sometimes.*

If Dr. Wallach found an instrument out of place or a bit of food not measuring up to his strict standards of kashruth, the offending item was not merely removed. Dr. Wallach usually flung it down on the hospital's hard stone floor, shouting in German all the while.

She remembered how Dr. Wallach had walked into the men's ward one night and found the man in charge dozing in his chair. Usually, when Dr. Wallach found something he didn't like, he would start to scream in German. That night, instead of screaming, Dr. Wallach found an interesting way of showing his displeasure. He quietly, very quietly, took off the man's shoes. Then he snuck away with them. The man spent the next day searching all over for the missing shoes. It was only after he'd admitted to what happened that the angry Dr. Wallach agreed to return them.

Thinking about her odd employer and wondering if, indeed, she had made a terrible error in coming to Jerusalem, Selma fell into a deep sleep.

When she awoke the next morning, Selma opened the shutters, as she always did. She had grown used to the strange sights that sometimes met her and no longer screamed when she saw a camel looking in. Today, though, the scene before her made her gasp in astonishment.

White! The quiet valley below her and the mountains beyond were white! Sparkling, beautiful white! Snow had fallen!

Selma couldn't help but feel excited. Snow was not unusual in her native land, but she knew that in Jerusalem it was a rare event.

"You'll finally get rest, Schvester Selma," Dr. Wallach told her when she went upstairs. "When it snows, this whole city shuts down. People stay home. Only the really sick are brave enough to go out. Perhaps we can relax a little. But be careful not to take your shoes off," he ended, his eyes twinkling.

Selma blushed a little. She remembered the hard thoughts she'd had the night before. Yes, Dr. Wallach was a little different from the stiff and formal doctors she had worked with in Germany. On the other hand, he was willing to laugh at himself. Yes, he demanded complete dedication from others, but he also demanded it of himself.

They had kept the huge front doors shut against the wind. Now they heard a loud knocking on it.

"It must be someone very ill to have come out today," Schvester Selma said as she hurried to answer the summons.

"Someone sick doesn't have the strength to bang like that," Dr. Wallach replied. "Let's go and see who is mad enough to walk through this snow."

They opened the door and found four men standing there. Their beards, usually black, were white, covered with a thick layer of frost.

"Come in! Come in!" Schvester Selma cried, astonished to see them. "Come and have something warm to drink."

"Thank you, Schvester, but we are here on urgent business," one of the men answered. "We must see Dr. Wallach."

"You can see him and still drink some tea," Dr. Wallach said, stepping into the hallway. "Here I am. And you," he said, staring at the men, "all look well to me."

"*Baruch Hashem*. We've not come because of illness."

"Wonderful! So it is the tea that brings you through this snow."

"No, not tea. Doctor, my brother needs you."

The doctor's face grew serious instantly. "He is sick?"

"No."

Dr. Wallach's famous temper began to ignite. "So why in the world are you here?" he shouted.

"A bris! The baby was born eight days ago. We live in Meah Shearim, all the family. We had all gotten together for the baby's bris, but the *mohel* never arrived. He lives in the Old City and is old and probably cannot walk all the way through this snow."

"While I am just a youngster who wants nothing more than to take an hour's hike through the freezing snow!" Dr. Wallach muttered. When he saw the men's faces fall, he laughed. "Now don't worry, your little nephew will get his bris on time if we have to get there on skis!" He turned to Schvester Selma. "This may take some time. Schvester, you are in charge here."

Selma glanced out the window. The flakes were dancing down from a sky as white as the sheets she in-

sisted on washing every day. The small stone poles the
people would hitch their donkeys to were completely
covered up. Dr. Wallach, like Selma herself, was very
small. Why, the snow would almost come up to his
knees!

Should she protest? Tell him that it was a dangerous,
mad thing to do? He could slip and break a leg, catch
pneumonia, or simply get lost in the falling snow! On
the other hand...

On the other hand, the first thing a nurse learned
was to obediently follow a doctor's orders. She knew
that if Dr. Wallach would not go, the baby would fail to
get his bris on time, an unthinkable thing. One final
thought went through her head: *If they needed you, Selma,
you wouldn't hesitate.*

Schvester Selma nodded. "Yes, Doctor. Only one thing…"

Dr. Wallach's eyes twinkled. He was expecting this little *schvester* to argue with him. There was nothing he enjoyed quite as much as a good fight!

"Perhaps you should take a long length of rope with you. You can each hold on to it. That way no one will get lost in the snow."

Disappointed, just a little, that his tiny nurse with the eyes that could blaze at him when she was angry had instead agreed without a murmur, Dr. Wallach slowly put on his dark coat with its soft fur collar.

Schvester Selma stared at the large men as they slowly battled their way through the snow. In their black jackets and hats, they looked like tiny dots of chocolate on a beautifully frosted white cake. She looked particularly at the upright figure of the doctor, so small beside his tall escorts.

"A big man," she murmured to himself. "Truly, a big man."

Suddenly Germany, and those quiet, well-behaved German doctors, didn't seem quite as appealing.

The baby room at the turn of the century

Chapter 6
Babies

Jerusalem, 1917

Schvester Selma stood before the heavy wooden door. She straightened her sparkling white apron and pulled her white cap more firmly down on her dark hair. Her shoulders, always straight, seemed to become even more firm. With a little shake she prepared to enter.

In all the hospital, this was the ward she loved the most — and the one she dreaded the most. This was the maternity ward, where new babies complainingly entered the world.

Selma loved the nursery where the newborns enjoyed the first vacation of their young lives. Swaddled closely in diapers, they looked out at the whitewashed walls surrounding them from tiny, red-rimmed eyes. Their little round lips and soft downy hair gave them the look of kittens: contented kittens, after their feeding, and angry kittens when they squeaked in hungry protest, waiting to be fed. Selma's heart went out to these helpless creatures. She glowed with happiness when a sickly infant grew bigger and began to gain weight properly. She would stay up all night, anxiously swabbing a feverish baby's forehead to keep the burning down. When a baby's labored breathing grew quieter until it breathed no more — unfortunately, not a rare occurrence in those days — Selma's lips would close tightly together as she comforted the crying mother.

Though she loved the maternity ward with its mewing little newborns, she also dreaded what she would find within. Though the hospital had become a cleaner and more effective place since Selma's arrival a year before, giving birth was still a difficult and dangerous business. Many mothers grew very ill after giving birth, and a good number actually died. Infections were common. Mothers who didn't have enough food to eat at home gave birth to tiny babies who were born sick.

Selma never knew quite what to expect when she walked through that wooden door. She remembered one woman who came in to the hospital one morning in terrible pain. Dr. Wallach examined her. "We've got to operate on you," he told the woman. "But don't worry, we'll save both you and your baby."

"I'm not worried," the woman answered. "But you'll have to wait a little while."

She spoke in hurried Yiddish to her anxious husband. He quickly ran from the room, a measuring tape in one hand.

"What is he doing?" Selma whispered, wondering if he was quite normal.

Dr. Wallach sighed. "He is measuring the distance between the operating table and the *aron kodesh* in the shul next door. He will then take a donkey cart to Kever Rachel, the tomb of our foremother, Rachel. He will cut a red thread the same size as that distance, go around the stone on the *kever* while holding it and reciting Tehillim. Then he will come back here on his donkey and attach one end of the thread to the bed and the other to the *aron*. Then and only then will they allow me to operate."

Selma was shocked. "Kever Rachel is in Bethlehem! That trip can take hours! I don't know if that baby will wait!"

"Oh, the baby will wait all right," Dr. Wallach said with a laugh. "Some call it superstition, while others believe in it completely. But the prayers always help, Schvester — I've never known a woman to give birth or to die while waiting for her red thread."

Indeed, this woman had given birth to a healthy baby boy whose wrist proudly bore a tiny bracelet of red thread.

When Schvester Selma entered the ward that day, she went straight to the bedside of a thin woman with a pale face. She was not very young, and her black eyes looked sad and hopeless. She had given birth to a little girl just yesterday, but she hardly had the strength to hold her new baby. The woman's mother worked downstairs in the hospital's laundry room. She had told Selma her daughter's story. Her husband and oldest son had been drafted by the Turks into the army. She was left alone with many young children. There was not enough to eat. There was not enough water to keep them clean. Already one young son had died.

Schvester Selma looked at the woman's sunken eyes and the dark circles beneath them. She spoke gently as she picked up her skinny hand to take her pulse. She thought of the woman's child, buried in the graveyard on the Mount of Olives. She thought of the new baby and the woman's other children. She sighed.

Dr. Wallach and Schvester Selma had stood by the woman yesterday while she had brought new life to the world. Now they stood by her again. This time there was no celebration of life. For just a day after giving birth, this mother died.

Selma tried to comfort the woman's weeping mother. "What will become of her baby?" the bereaved mother wailed. "No mother, her father so far away! I have six little ones still at home, and my husband is sick! Now we must take in my daughter's other children. We can't take care of a newborn properly."

"We will find a woman to nurse the infant," Selma assured her quietly. "Now come, you must go to the little ones at home."

Selma did everything efficiently. She found a woman in the hospital who had just given birth. She arranged for her to nurse the poor motherless infant as well as her own. In the days that followed, Selma made certain that the new baby was bathed and held.

But, she thought to herself, *what will become of the little one? How long can she stay here?*

Though she had so much to do, Selma found herself often simply staring at the tiny, red-faced child. With her mother dead and her father gone to fight a war he cared nothing about, the grandparents had the job of naming the baby. "Samoocha will be her name," they announced.

"A good choice," Dr. Wallach said when he heard.

"What does it mean?" Selma asked curiously.

"It comes from the word *simchah*, which means 'joy.' She's had enough sorrow, certainly, in her first days on this earth."

A few days later, the doctor again found his head nurse near little Samoocha's crib. "You seem interested in the child," he said to Schvester Selma.

"She's so helpless. No mother or father to care for her."

"Schvester..."

Schvester Selma looked at the doctor. Strange, Dr. Wallach was having a difficult time choosing his words. He usually had no problem speaking with her.

"Doctor, is anything wrong?"

"No. Samoocha's grandmother has asked us something."

"What?" Why was Dr. Wallach taking so long to get to the point?

"He's asked me to keep the baby. Adopt her."

Selma's eyes widened. "You?" she blurted out. Then she blushed for her rude outburst. But the idea was so strange. Dr. Wallach was not married. A housekeeper took care of his small apartment near the hospital. Between the hospital and the patients in the city, Dr. Wallach was hardly ever at home. How in the world could he take care of a little girl?

Dr. Wallach looked at his head nurse, standing so straight next to him. "Yes, me — and you, Schvester."

Selma's astonishment increased. "Me?"

"The child can stay here in the hospital. I can make certain that she receives food and medical care. However, as she grows older she will need someone who will take full responsibility for her. A mother. Schvester, can you do it?"

In the few years she'd been in Jerusalem, Selma had faced many surprises. Yet nothing had quite prepared her for this.

If I agree, she thought to herself, *then I must stay here. Do I want to?*

Selma's mind raced. She thought about the dirt and poverty of the city. She thought of the neat, clean, orderly hallways of the Salomon Heine Hospital, the Hamburg hospital where she'd worked before this. She thought about camels and red strings and muddy sidewalks where she had already lost two pairs of boots. She thought about Dr. Wallach, with his endless shouting and bad temper.

When she'd arrived, Seima had signed a three-year contract with the hospital. That contract was almost finished. She could return to Hamburg. To civilization.

Little Samoocha gave a whimper, which grew into an angry yowl. She was hungry. A nurse came over and picked her up.

Selma had always wanted to give to others. She remembered her head nurse in Hamburg speaking of the orphans of Jerusalem.

Hamburg seemed very far away. Very clean — and very, very far away.

"I think you're right, Dr. Wallach," she said crisply. "We can take care of the baby."

Within a few years, little Samoocha was joined by Bolissa. Bolissa's father had come from Syria, carrying his little baby with him. Her mother had died on the way. Now he stood before Dr. Wallach. Schvester Selma, as was her way, sat quietly in a corner nearby.

"Please," the man pleaded. "I have no money. No place to stay. I can't take care of her. She's a good little girl. I have heard that you have done this before."

A little smile played on Selma's lips. It seemed Samoocha's story had reached as far as Syria!

Dr. Wallach looked at her. "Well?" he demanded.

Selma nodded. "We will take care of her."

And so Bolissa joined the unusual family growing up at Wallach's Hospital.

General E. H. Allenby in Jerusalem

Chapter 7

A New Master

Jerusalem, 1917

Boom!

The explosion sent gravel and dirt flying into the open window of the hospital. It also sent most of the patients, and some of the staff, into a panic.

"Help! We're all being killed!" shrieked a young nursing assistant.

"Ima! I don't want to die!" a patient with a white bandage draped loosely on his red hair shouted.

"They're coming! They're coming!" an elderly man sitting in the waiting room groaned.

Boom! Another explosion rocked the area. The screams and cries grew louder.

Schvester Selma hurried up from her basement room. She had been awake all last night, helping in the hospital's operating room. The battlefield had grown closer to them, and all yesterday men torn and bleeding had been carried in. There was a young Turkish boy with a bullet lodged in his shoulder. Two soldiers whose filthy uniforms hid terrible scars from bayonets. A Yiddish-speaking man who'd been drafted and who limped in, his ankle broken. There was even a British soldier or two who had managed to get past the Turkish guns and stagger in looking for help.

Schvester Selma and Dr. Wallach worked on each soldier, not caring whose side he was on or whose uniform he was wearing. Selma had ripped off torn clothing to look for the wounds. She'd bandaged bleeding arms and legs and wiped the sweat off feverish brows. She'd handed the doctor endless instruments as he did emergency operations. She'd calmed down terrified young boys who'd been hurt, giving them tea or brandy. She'd held the hands of the dying, taking their names and promising to write to their mothers. Though most didn't understand the German she spoke, they could feel the comfort in her voice and smiled weakly through their pain.

When the number of wounded grew too great, Selma and her fellow workers cleared the room downstairs where the dead were usually kept until burial and used it for more stricken soldiers. So many wounded! So much pain and blood! In the middle of the terrible day, a new baby decided to make her appearance in the world, and she, too, had to be washed, swaddled, and comforted. Birth and death, blood and tea. It had been a long day.

Finally, in the early hours of the morning, Selma had allowed her weary feet to take her to bed. Now, only two hours later, she'd been woken by the terrible roar of guns and the even more frightening screams of patients. They were under attack!

The world had been at war now for four years. The Great War, many called it, the war to end all wars. Three empires — the German, Austro-Hungarian, and Turkish — had banded together to fight off many other countries, including England, France, and the United States.

As a loyal German citizen, Selma knew that she should hope her country would be the victor, but as a nurse, and as a Jew, all Selma wanted was an end to the terrible bloodshed. So many young men killed and wounded! So many families left to starve here in Jerusalem, while their fathers and brothers were taken against their will to fight a war they had no interest in.

Selma had already been in Palestine for two years. All through those years, as she and Dr. Wallach tried to make the hospital a clean and efficient place, they had suffered from the war so far away. Able-bodied men were often taken by the Turks and thrown into the army. The generals didn't care that these men were fathers of large families. So what if a Jerusalem child would starve? There was a Great War going on! Sometimes the war caused shortages of medicines, bandages, and even food. The soldiers had to have supplies! Once, the hospital received a large shipment of bandages from Jewish supporters in Germany. To Selma's astonishment, Dr.

Wallach ordered them to be put into boxes and buried in the garden behind the hospital!

"Bandages in the dirt? This is insanity!" the head nurse protested.

"The Schvester should not worry," Dr. Wallach's eyes twinkled. "I've double-wrapped them."

"Does the doctor think they will sprout and grow more bandages?" Selma retorted.

"No, I will be satisfied if we can keep this year's crop," Dr. Wallach answered. "Just wait and see."

"I'll wait. But this is not how we did things in Germany."

"You're not in Germany now, Schvester. Germany is very far away."

Sure enough, the next day two Turkish colonels walked in and demanded a large supply of bandages to take to the front. Dr. Wallach declared — with perfect truth — that he had none to spare here in the hospital. He politely allowed the suspicious officers to search through every closet and drawer.

When they left, empty-handed and disgruntled, he turned to Selma. "You see, Schvester, what a harvest we will reap when we go to unbury our treasure."

Selma couldn't help but smile. "The doctor is right," she laughed. "Germany is very far away."

Until now, though the war caused them problems, the battlefields were far away. It was only lately that the people of Jerusalem had actually seen wounded. And now they themselves were under attack!

When she walked into the ward, Schvester Selma could hear the babble of languages. People were shouting in Yiddish, Hebrew, Turkish, German, Russian, and Polish. The little nurse from Germany looked around her at the overcrowded ward. This would never do. If someone didn't do something soon, pandemonium would break out. Someone had to stop it. Someone...

Selma put her hands calmly on her hips. Well, Dr. Wallach wasn't the only one who knew how to raise his voice. "Silence!" she shouted.

Strangely enough, the room grew quiet.

"You, Ari," she said, pointing at a stocky Iraqi Jew who worked in the kitchen, "go find Dr. Wallach. I believe he may be in the synagogue for Shabbat morning services. Tell him the hospital is under attack."

Another shell fell nearby. The explosion left Selma's ears ringing. She made a quick decision. "Srulik, we're going down to the basement," she barked to a black-bearded man who smelled of onions, who was in charge of hospital supplies. "It will be safer there."

"The basement? Who?"

"Everyone. Get the staff organized. You'll have to bring the patients. Those who can walk should. Those who can't must be carried on stretchers. Put mattresses on the floor. Keep the newborns warm." The orders were coming thick and fast.

Another explosion. Suddenly, the air grew white and thick. "Gas! They're shooting poison gas!" Dudu screamed. Two little boys with dysentery started to wail.

Schvester Selma gave a cautious sniff. She'd heard terrible tales of the mustard gas that had been used during battles, how it burned the skin and eyes and left people helpless. Could it be...?

And then the little nurse started to laugh. "It's not gas," she said, running her finger through the white dust. "It's flour! They must have hit the storage room." Sure enough, Srulik came flying into the door, almost in tears over the destruction of his beloved supply room.

Schvester Selma sternly told him to calm down and help get the patients downstairs. Though relieved that the threat of deadly mustard gas had turned into flour, she knew that there still was danger. Danger to the staff and, more important, to the patients who were her responsibility.

Within the hour, the entire hospital had moved to the basement. It was a strange Shabbat they spent down there. There was little water, and it soon grew hot and stuffy. The children were frightened and cried constantly. Selma was used to working under difficult conditions. Today, though, she found it hard to ignore that creeping little fear of battle and bloodshed that was making its way through her. The explosions were coming close, so close! But she didn't have much time to feel afraid. Not with newborns to be fed, children to be calmed, wounded to be tended. Whenever she had a quiet moment or two and began to feel nervous, she simply remembered how mustard gas had turned into flour and began to laugh once again.

After a day that seemed endless, Dr. Wallach made Havdalah in the basement. The flickering candle cast strange shadows on the dark walls. As Selma listened to the cries of the patients wishing each other a happy week, she wondered just what the week would bring. Tomorrow night, she knew, was the first day of Chanukah. Dr. Wallach had spoken of the miracles that had taken place in this very city, so many years ago. Now Jerusalem indeed needed a miracle.

Schvester Selma, and all of Jerusalem, found out the very next day that miracles could still happen here.

Dawn comes quietly to Jerusalem, with only the birds announcing its arrival. That Sunday morning the city seemed especially still. Some time in the middle of the night, the horrible sound of shelling had stopped. What could it mean?

One of the nurse's aides crept slowly out of the basement. He couldn't bear another minute of the stuffy, dusty air. Carefully he stepped out onto the street.

Within minutes he was back. He came in at a run, shouting. Even Dr. Wallach, who didn't like such behavior in his hospital (he felt, after all, that only he had the right to yell) did not stop him.

"It's over! It's over!" the nurse's aide screamed.

"What?"

"Over?"

"What's going on?"

Everyone had something to say, something to ask.

"The white flag is flying from the roof of Ezrat Nashim Hospital. I've seen British troops walking through the streets. The Turks have surrendered!"

Everyone who could stand up on his own two feet did. Some people laughed, others cried. This terrible war, which had caused such suffering, was over in Palestine at last!

Schvester Selma had mixed feelings. After all, she was a loyal German, and the Turks were fighting together with her countrymen. But two years of living under Turkish rule had shown her how corrupt they were. Nothing in this country got done without bribery and favoritism. More than once she'd heard from Dr. Wallach of how he had saved this Jew or that Jew from the draft or punishment, or even death, because he'd paid off some Turkish official. The British, she hoped, would be better rulers.

In any case, the bloodshed and starvation were coming to an end. A miracle, indeed!

War's end or not, Selma was not one to forget her responsibilities. The patients had spent almost twenty-four hours in this terrible basement. Peace was here and that was fine. Now she had to get them back upstairs.

The hospital had just about returned to normal when suddenly four uniformed officers strode boldly through the doors. Selma watched anxiously as they walked into the small room that served as Dr. Wallach's office. From their uniforms it was clear that these were British soldiers.

Selma and Dr. Wallach were German nationals. Could it be that they were going to be taken prisoner?

The moments moved slowly, so slowly. More officers marched into the office. How many did they need to arrest a few doctors and nurses?

Suddenly Dr. Wallach motioned to his nurse. For once he was subdued. He spoke quietly. Selma's face lit up. "Certainly, Doctor. At once."

She raced into her room and carefully pulled out a set of china dishes. She kept these for the richer patients, knowing it would cause them pain to eat off the plain plates the hospital usually used. With hands shaking slightly, she prepared tea and cut a few pieces of cake left over from Shabbat. Carefully, she laid out the food on a small table in the hospital's parlor.

General Allenby

Not long afterwards, little Schvester Selma of Hamburg watched as General Allenby, British conqueror of Jerusalem, walked into the hospital. He was followed by several Turkish officials and Jamil Pasha, the Turkish mayor of Jerusalem. A Turkish officer who looked pale and white and had a large scar on his forehead walked behind them carrying a sword. Somberly, he handed the sword over to the British general.

The battle was over, and the Turkish officials, including the mayor of Jerusalem, were here in Wallach's Hospital, the largest building in the area, to surrender the city. Schvester Selma, speaking French, graciously poured out the first decent cup of tea General Allenby had enjoyed in many days.

When the general had turned on his heel and left, the *schvester* ran to her supplies to tend the cut on the head of the defeated officer. Enough of history: there was nursing to be done.

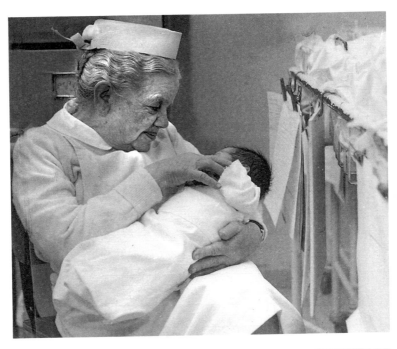

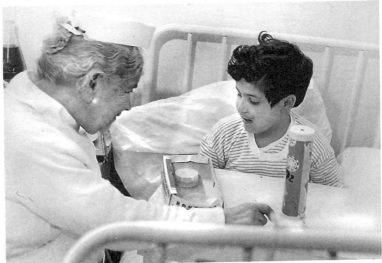

Shvester Selma and her children

Chapter 8

Return to Germany

Germany, 1923

The years pass quickly when a person is busy. In these six years that Schvester Selma had spent in Jerusalem, she had been very, very busy.

The war's end had brought some changes to the hospital. Selma often remembered, with a smile, the way her old friend Dudu had behaved immediately after the British had taken charge.

Dr. Wallach had been shouting at someone. At whom, and for what, Selma couldn't remember. After all, Dr. Wallach was always shouting at someone. At least, when he wasn't saving a patient's life or doing someone a favor.

Suddenly, Dudu had burst into the room. Selma watched, amazed, as the dark-haired cleaning woman stood before the doctor.

"The Englishmen have been here. They told me that we are now living in a democracy. You are a person. I am a person. You work a little and earn a lot. I work a lot and earn a little. That is the only difference between us. So stop shouting!"

In the hospital, the joke went that Schvester Selma would notice a pin that had fallen on the floor. Well, now the hospital was so quiet that if a pin had really dropped, you would have heard it fall. Someone — a lowly cleaning woman — had stood up to Dr. Wallach. If a hospital worker made even the tiniest mistake, the doctor used to scream and shout. What would he do now?

Selma stood tensely nearby. She was ready to try and calm down the doctor. Dudu had a big mouth, but she had a big family, too. If Dr. Wallach fired Dudu, how would her children eat?

Dr. Wallach stared at his employee. For a moment, he was silent. Then he opened his mouth and roared with laughter. He didn't say a word to his disrespectful washerwoman. He just laughed and laughed and laughed.

As Schvester Selma told the workers to get back to their jobs, she couldn't help but think of what a strange, unexpected man her boss was.

But aside from Dudu's outburst, life after the war's end had grown easier. There was more food and more medicine. The British built a pipeline to bring more water to the city. The terrible epidemics ended. Selma was finally given a room of her own. She had her very own sink in one corner, a real luxury in Jerusalem. She kept her room very neat and very comfortable. Nurses and doctors and even the cleaning staff would come to her with their questions and problems. To all, she would serve a cup of tea and some biscuits and give advice in her quiet, pleasant voice.

Yes, they had been six busy but satisfying years. Now Selma knew what she had to do next.

"You want to go where?" Dr. Wallach's voice, never soft at the best of times, had turned into a scream.

"To Hamburg, Doctor."

"Hamburg? Nonsense. What have you got to do in Hamburg?"

Selma's voice was soft but firm. "Hamburg is my home."

"Home? Home? Jerusalem is home!"

Selma felt a pang of doubt. Was the doctor right? Had this impoverished city become her home? She ignored the feeling. "My contract gives me the right to a trip back to Germany every three years. It is six years since I have arrived."

Dr. Wallach grew silent. Six years since this young woman had arrived. In six years, she'd managed to do what no other nurse had: make his hospital an efficient and yet caring place. Six years. So many hours they'd worked side by side, fighting off death and disease. Was she to leave now? Go back to Hamburg?

His voice softened. "And what about the children?

Schvester, what of the children?"

Selma didn't need Dr. Wallach's reminder. Indeed, she had lain awake for many nights, worrying about leaving little Samoocha and Bolissa. The girls had the best medical care Jerusalem could offer. They drank milk from the hospital's own herd of cows kept in a shed in the back. They were both growing up healthy and

Shaare Zedek's own milk supplies

strong. Selma loved to watch them play. The thought of leaving them was very hard. But Selma had grown up in a world where people did not show what they were feeling. She wouldn't speak of her emotions. Particularly not to this infuriating doctor of hers!

Selma stared back at him. Her face was stony. "I've

seen to it that they will be taken care of."

Dr. Wallach spoke with harsh formality. "If the Schvester insists on leaving her responsibility..."

"The Schvester insists on having her contract fulfilled."

"When will the Schvester return to us?"

"I will send a wire." With that, Schvester Selma turned away. But Dr. Wallach's voice followed her. "Remember, Schvester Selma, this is your home."

Why am I returning to Hamburg? Selma asked herself the question as she carefully folded her black suit into her trunk.

Selma herself didn't know the answer to her question. She didn't have very much family in Germany. She loved the work here in Jerusalem, and she loved the people. And the babies.

Yet Palestine wasn't Germany. Germany was cultured and clean. And quiet. Here everyone spoke quickly and loudly. Everyone argued. Everyone (even Dudu!) thought she or he knew best. Sometimes Selma longed for the courteous manners and dignity of her homeland.

"I need a little time to think. About who I am and where I belong. That's why I'm going." With those words, she firmly pushed the trunk shut.

Hamburg had changed since Selma had last been there. In the years that she'd been gone, Germany had lost the war it had fought. Strangely, there was a new government in charge. The Kaiser, Germany's former ruler, was gone. After his defeat, he'd run away to the Netherlands. Times were hard. There was much poverty.

Some things, though, had stayed the same. In Germany, *Herr Doktor*, the doctor, was treated with respect, almost with awe. To a nurse, the doctor's word was law. Once, Selma had thought that to be a very good thing, but that was before she'd come to Jerusalem...

Selma remembered one day in Jerusalem when she'd sent a young nurse down to Dr. Wallach with a list of medicines she needed. It was Dr. Wallach's job to approve all requests for medicines. The list included ten headache pills. "Schvester Selma needs those pills for herself," the young nurse explained to Dr. Wallach.

Dr. Wallach gave her a fierce look. "Tell the Schvester that she should not be taking so many pills for headaches," he said.

The young nurse, shy and embarrassed, relayed Dr. Wallach's answer to Schvester Selma. Selma laughed. "Tell the doctor that if I have headaches, he is the cause!" she said.

Selma got her pills.

Now, in Hamburg, Selma wondered what would happen if she had dared to speak to a German doctor like that. Dr. Wallach shouted. He made demands. But he had a sense of humor. And oddly enough, he loved when people stood up to him.

Selma remembered another story of her eccentric doctor. A woman once came to the hospital after visiting hours were over. She found a man guarding the entrance. "Please, all I ask is five minutes to see my husband. He was operated on yesterday. But be quick, before that crazy Wallach comes."

The guard gave her a smile and pulled open the gate, reminding her to come back in five minutes.

Not long afterwards, the woman returned. She thanked the guard many times for his good deed. "What is your name?" she asked him before she left.

"My name?" The man gave another smile. "I'm that crazy Wallach," he said.

Other things about Hamburg also seemed strange to Selma. She stared at the symbols of Christianity which hung over all the beds in the hospital where she'd worked. When she'd been there before she had hardly noticed them. Now it seemed odd to be in a place where there were no mezuzot on the doors. And the food? Milk cooked with meat, stews made from who knew what kind of animal! In Jerusalem, Dr. Wallach was incredibly strict about the kashruth of his hospital. Everything had to be under the most careful kashruth supervision. The hospital even kept its own cows, because Dr. Wallach wanted to be sure the milk he was serving was *chalav Yisrael*.

When she'd first arrived in Jerusalem, Selma had thought his care rather strange. The home she had come from was not as religious as this. Now she respected his dedication to his ideals. She saw how important it was to many of her patients. "The kashruth of the kitchen is as important as the cleanliness of the operating room," she used to tell her staff.

Yes, Hamburg had changed since Selma had left it. But, she realized, so had she.

For three months, Selma stayed in Europe. She enjoyed the culture. She loved seeing friends and family. She traveled to museums and read books. She ate good German food, stuff that wasn't cooked in olive oil and prepared with sharp, odd-tasting spices.

When three months were over, she gratefully sent her wire to Jerusalem. "Arriving next month." She was going home.

Love to all

Chapter 9

Nursing

Jerusalem, 1923–1929

W hen Selma returned to her adopted city, life settled down into a routine, though nothing was ever really routine in the stone walls of Wallach's Hospital. In most hospitals, the head nurse was in charge of all the other nurses. She made sure they did their jobs properly and the patients got the care they needed. Schvester Selma did much more than that. Many years later, she said, "From 1920 to 1930 I was responsible for everything from heaven to earth."

In those days, after an operation a person stayed in bed for an entire week. In Wallach's Hospital, the policy was that when he would get out of bed and take his first steps, there was always someone next to him to help him up and make sure he was well enough to stand. That someone was Schvester Selma.

If a man was too sick to even get to the hospital, Dr. Wallach would race to his house to see what was wrong. Someone rode next to the doctor in his donkey cart, holding a kerosene lamp to light up the darkness. That someone was Schvester Selma.

When a woman was about to give birth, a woman trained in such matters was supposed to help her. This trained woman was called a midwife. Unfortunately, often the midwife couldn't get to the hospital on time. Wallach's Hospital was at the edge of the city, and most midwives didn't live nearby. There was certainly never enough money to hire a carriage.

Since babies don't like to wait to be born, if the midwife wasn't there, someone had to help deliver the baby. That someone was Schvester Selma.

There are some diseases one person can quickly catch from another. When many, many people are struck by these illnesses, it is called an epidemic. When Schvester Selma first came to Jerusalem, the city suffered terribly from such epidemics, with hundreds and hundreds of people getting the same illnesses. Sometimes every person in a family was sick at the same time.

Shaare Zedek had Jerusalem's only isolation wards. These are hospital wards where people who suffer from contagious diseases are sent. The idea is to make them well while, at the same time, make certain they can't infect anyone else with their germs.

If Selma was busy taking care of the operating

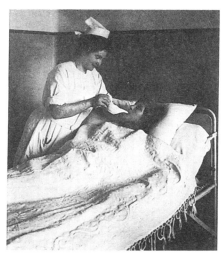

The isolation ward

ooms, the babies, and her house calls, it was the isola-
ion wards that really kept her running. There were two
nits, one for diptheria and one for typhoid. They were
ocated in a small building next to the hospital. Though
hey had no running water or pipes, everything had to be
ept absolutely clean. Because they didn't want the
urses to carry out the germs from the isolation wards
nd into the city, each nurse assigned there lived there
or a full month and was not allowed to leave. To make it
asier, the isolation nurses were given special food. Still,
t could get very boring, being in the same building for
our weeks at a time!

When a patient was brought into the isolation unit
e was given a hospital uniform. His clothing, and all
lothing that was worn in the ward, were soaked in horri-
le-smelling chemicals for a full twenty-four hours to kill

any germs that were on them. They were then dried and returned to the sick person. The patients had to be kept clean, and some needed more than one bath a day. The only bathtubs in the isolation units were metal tubs on wheels. These were rolled out to the main building to be filled with hot water, then rolled back into the ward.

Of course, no visitors were allowed into the isolation wards, so it was up to the nurses to keep the sick people cheered up. Unfortunately, children, especially, seemed to get contagious diseases. The nurses would hold up the young people to the windows so they could see their mothers, fathers, brothers, and sisters.

Shaare Zedek's isolation wards were always very busy, because they were the only such wards in the entire city. Someone had to see to it that all the patients received proper care and at the same time were not able to make anyone else sick.

That someone was — of course — Schvester Selma. Dressed in a special uniform that covered her regular one, she would visit the isolation wards every day to make certain all was doing well.

Slowly, as the years passed, the hospital grew bigger and more efficient. More doctors were hired. The small kerosene stoves were replaced by huge gas ovens. Food, bandages, and medicines were more available and of better quality.

All of that progress was to be tested on one terrible night in 1929.

The day was drawing to an end. Schvester Selma sat at her desk filling out some forms. Mrs. Levi in bed 2 was running a temperature. Selma would have to ask Dr. Wallach if she should be given more medication. Mr. Sabato was looking better. Tomorrow, Selma would tell his daughter he could go home. The newly born twins were...

Selma's thoughts were interrupted by the sound of footsteps clattering down the stone floors. She glanced at her silver watch. Nine-thirty. Who could it be, so late?

Selma walked out of her room. One look at what was awaiting her sent her into a run. There, on a stretcher, lay a young man, his head shiny with oozing blood. Next to him stood two young men, their own faces white.

Questions could come later. Schvester Selma barked a few orders. Soon doctors, nurses, and orderlies were racing to the operating room.

While the patient was being carried in, the door opened once again. Like some kind of nightmare that wouldn't go away, there in front of Selma stood two more pale-faced young men carrying a stretcher. On that stretcher — again — lay a bloody form.

No, questions could not wait. What was going on?

Selma had been in Palestine for thirteen years now. Though her Hebrew had improved a lot, she couldn't make out a word of what the young man who'd carried the stretcher in was saying. He was speaking quickly, almost hysterically.

"What is it?" Selma asked a nurse who was speaking

with the stretcher-bearer.

The nurse's eyes were filled with tears. "They've come from Hebron. There's been a pogrom there. A massacre. They don't know how many are dead. The British have put up roadblocks, but our people are smuggling in the wounded anyway."

Selma's lips tightened. She was not interested in politics. She was more interested in keeping people well. But even she knew that relations between the Arabs and the Jews were not very good now. The British, who ruled Palestine, were supposed to keep the peace, but they were not doing a very good job of it. From the looks of it, they were doing a very poor job, indeed.

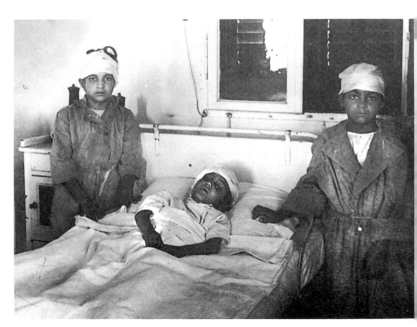

Victims of the Hebron massacre

As the night wore on, Selma saw people with terrible knife wounds. She saw young men beaten black and blue and old rabbis breathing their last breath. In Arabic, Hebron was known as El-Khalil, which means "the friend." On this terrible day, there had been no friendship in Hebron, at least not for its tiny community of Jews. There were about seven hundred Jews living in the city among eighteen thousand Arabs. In a well-planned action, the Arabs had attacked the Jews. The wounded were all brought to Jerusalem. Some were brought to the newly opened Hadassah Hospital, while others came under the healing hands of Dr. Wallach and Schvester Selma.

By the time the night was over, sixty-seven Jews were dead. The terrible Hebron massacre had become a part of Jewish history.

The sun began to rise over the city. It bathed the stone walls of Shaare Zedek hospital in a pink glow. Inside, Schvester Selma slowly washed her hands clean of blood. She was exhausted. She'd been up all night, helping in the operating room. All she wanted, now, was to go to bed.

She thought of the patients waiting for her. Babies had to be tended to, medicine had to be given. It was another day to tend to the sick. Bed would just have to wait.

One of Schvester Selma's nursing school classes

Chapter 10

The Nurse Becomes a Teacher

Jerusalem, 1946

"The old one is on the loose."
"The old one is on the loose."
"Pssst. Get moving. The old one is on the loose."

Thirty years had passed since young Schvester Selma had hesitantly stepped off the train onto the muddy Jerusalem street. In thirty years Jerusalem had grown enormously. Shaare Zedek Hospital had grown enormously. Tiny Schvester Selma, too, had grown. Not in height — she was just as short and just as straight-backed as ever. But the young nurse had become a well-known Jerusalem personality, beloved by all who had passed through her hospital.

In 1934, eighteen years after her arrival, the nurse

became a teacher. Shaare Zedek, growing and needing more and more nursing help, had opened its own nursing school. Schvester Selma stood at its head, teaching the girls all the practical things they would need to know to become professional and caring nurses. Now, in the year 1946, little Schvester Selma was known by her students as "the old one." When the old one was on the loose, you ran to do whatever you were supposed to be doing. The old one was caring. She was loving. But oh was she ever strict!

Esther, one of the students who joined the nursing school that year, knew all about Schvester Selma's strictness. This was the year after the terrible Holocaust that had taken place in Europe had ended. Like many of the nursing students, Esther was a refugee. Her parents had been killed by the Nazis. She had no home of her own. She had nothing but the little basement room she shared with her friend Miriam, also a refugee.

It wasn't easy, being a nursing student. The girls were given one half-day off a week. If things got busy and the patients needed them, the students lost even this short vacation!

Esther had looked forward to her Friday half-day off for many days. It had been a long, hard winter, and she hadn't had a vacation day in three months. She ran down to her basement room to pack up a few things. Suddenly, Schvester Selma's assistant, Margit, appeared. "You'd better get some sleep, Esther," she said. "We need you to do special nursing duty tonight."

Esther groaned. Night duty was absolutely the worst! You sat next to a patient who usually slept. The hospital was dark and silent. You couldn't read. You couldn't talk. You certainly couldn't sleep! It was twelve hours of the most incredible boredom a person could imagine.

"I'm going out now," Esther said, trying to sound calm. "I can't do night duty tonight. Tell someone else."

"Schvester Selma said you should take it."

"Well, tell the Schvester I refuse."

Even as she said the words, Esther regretted them. Refuse Schvester Selma? Schvester Selma, who managed at the same time to be so strict and yet so kind? Who demanded so much of them — but demanded more of herself? With pale face and pounding heart, Esther turned to the small suitcase on her bed, but the joy was gone. She'd refused Schvester Selma. What would happen now?

Within minutes, Margit was back. "Schvester Selma has asked that you come to her room."

Like most everyone in the hospital, Esther had spent some time in Schvester Selma's small room next to the maternity ward. It was always kept absolutely spotless. It contained a bed, a few beautiful pictures on the wall, some books, a table, and chairs. At that table Schvester Selma would pour out cups of mint tea, while others poured out their hearts to her. Doctors and patients and nursing students all found their way there to speak to the *schvester*. Esther had always enjoyed her meetings with Schvester Selma. What would the head nurse say to her now?

As the minutes of her precious half-day holiday ticked by, Esther sat by the table and listened to Schvester Selma. For two hours Selma spoke to her about nursing. The words were so inspiring that Esther could remember them over fifty years later!

"Those who come to us need help," Selma said to her. "If you are a nurse, a true nurse, that is what you are there for."

"I know that," Esther gulped, "but it's hard."

"Hard? Yes, hard. At the same time, it is the most rewarding thing a woman can do."

Schvester Selma poured another cup of inky tea. She peered at Esther. "You take two spoons of sugar, yes?"

"Yes. But how did you know?"

"That is my business, Esther. If you walk into a room with six patients, and one of them says she does not take sugar in her tea, when you give her tea the next day you must remember that. If you care enough, you will remember. To help and to heal — this is what we live for."

Schvester Selma stood up and walked to her bookshelf. She pulled down a small volume. "Read it," she demanded.

Esther stared at the words before her. It was a short poem:

> *I slept and dreamt*
> *that life was joy*
> *I awoke and saw*
> *that life was duty*
> *I acted and behold*
> *duty was joy*

"This, my dear, is my motto, the motto of all nurses. Duty and responsibility. This is our life. Our joy."

"But it's hard, Schvester, so hard. We have no free time. Dr. Wallach doesn't allow us to leave at night. I need a life of my own sometimes."

Schvester Selma looked at the young girl with compassion. She knew all too well how difficult this was — the work, the aching feet, the lack of decent facilities. She also knew that dedication was the only way to make a real nurse.

"Esther, I cannot force you to do this. If you're not prepared to do it, go and pack. Leave us. A nurse who can't give up her own personal enjoyment for a patient will never be a nurse."

Esther slowly walked back to her room and unpacked her bag. Not because she was afraid of being thrown out of the nursing school, but because the words of a short poem, and the words of a tiny nurse, had imprinted themselves in her heart.

A few hours later, Esther had a glimpse of what Schvester Selma was trying to tell her. The night duty proved to be anything but boring. The woman she was watching began to have her baby. This infant was in no rush to make an appearance, though, and the woman was in great pain. Esther, still fairly new, didn't know what to do. While the doctors and midwives and nurses surrounded the patient, Esther simply held her hand. Sometimes, when the pain grew bad, the woman would squeeze until Esther's fingers burned, but she said nothing. When beads of sweat appeared on the patient's brow, Esther quietly wet a rag and rubbed her forehead with it.

Later, much later, when the baby was finally born with a squawk and a yell, the new mother looked at the student nurse. "You know, from among all those who surrounded me, you were the most important," she said, giving a weak but grateful smile.

It was, Esther remembers five decades later, one of the most satisfying moments of her life. "Behold, duty was joy."

The nursing students worked six and a half days a week and took classes, too. When needed, they also worked the night shift. For pay, they were given a white uniform with a starched collar and thick gray stockings. They were also assigned tiny rooms and given meals three times a day. (Woe to the one who was late and missed dinnertime! She went hungry.) All this, plus the princely sum of ninety grush a month.

Just how much was ninety grush in those days? Esther's roommate, Miriam, was lucky. Most of her family had survived the war. Her parents were in Belgium, her grandfather in London. She had three surviving brothers: one in New York, one in Paris, and one in England. Ninety grush was just about enough to pay for stamps for the letters Miriam would send to her family. When Miriam wanted to buy a luxury — a new toothbrush, for instance, or a pair of shoes — she took extra work in other hospitals to make the necessary cash. Still, she didn't complain. She wasn't starving, and she was learning to become a nurse. What could be better?

Like Esther, Miriam, too, learned more from Schvester Selma than merely the proper way to bandage a wound or give a shot. Once, the hospital was particularly busy. For almost two months, the nursing students had been doing extra duty. One day, Schvester Selma pulled Miriam out of her classroom.

"I just got a phone call from Haifa," she said. "Your friend David is getting married tonight."

Miriam smiled. David, like she, had survived the war. He and Miriam had been together during the first difficult days of aliyah to Israel. How nice that he was getting married! But what did Schvester Selma have to do with it?

"He left a message for you. He would like you to attend the wedding."

Miriam's face fell. The hospital was still very busy. No way she would be allowed to leave.

"Go and pack up. Get back by tomorrow afternoon."

Miriam stared. What had Schvester Selma said?

"But...but I'm in middle of a class. And night shift..."

Schvester Selma looked at her sternly. "Miriam, this is important. A boy is getting married, and he has no family to attend his wedding. You've got to go."

As Miriam sat on the slow, slow bus to Haifa, she mulled over the lesson she had just learned. To take off a day for enjoying herself — impossible. To help another? That was her duty. That was her joy.

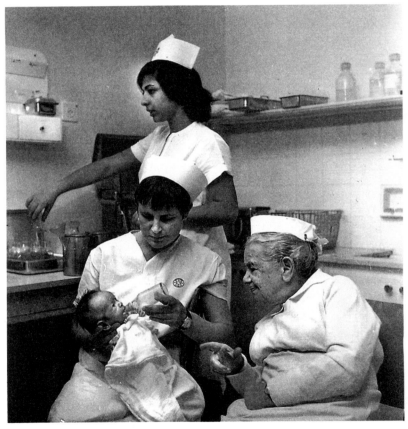

Years later, Shvester Selma continued to teach and guide new nurses

War of Independence — a direct hit

Chapter 11

Tragedy

Jerusalem, 1947

The dark-skinned, pretty young woman glanced at her wristwatch. Already 6:45! If she didn't hurry, she would be late in arriving at the WIZO Day Care Center where she worked. She liked her job as a helper in the center too much to take a chance on getting fired for lateness. Besides, she knew the importance of being on time and being responsible. After all, she'd had the best teacher in the world to show her.

Bolissa knocked on the sparkling white door. It led to the room she liked the most in the whole world. When the door flew open, she gave the woman inside a warm smile. This was the woman she loved more than any other in the whole world. This was the woman who had taken her off a camel and into her arms. This was

Schvester Selma, Bolissa's foster mother, who had raised her for so many years right here in the hallways of Wallach's Hospital.

More than twenty years had passed since Bolissa's father had left his baby in the care of Dr. Wallach and his head nurse, Schvester Selma. In those years Bolissa had grown up. Now she was a lovely young woman whom any mother would be proud of. Like her foster mother, she also hoped for a career helping people. She was working as an assistant in a day care center, caring for the infants.

After bidding Selma a warm yet respectful farewell, Bolissa started to leave the hospital. In a corridor she met Margit, Schvester Selma's assistant. Margit hesitated for a moment. She wanted to talk to Bolissa about something. Perhaps now was the time? No, it was already getting late. It wasn't that important anyway. It could wait for tomorrow.

But sometimes, for some people, tomorrow never comes.

It had been thirty years since the terrible sound of exploding bullets had been heard in the hallways of Shaare Zedek. That had been during those last awful days of the First World War. Today the muffled thud and thump was heard once again. The meaning of the boom that split the quiet morning air was unmistakable. It was twenty minutes after seven on a cold but sunny Jerusalem morning in February.

Shaare Zedek was now a modern hospital, and it

boasted a fine telephone system. Thus, it didn't take more than a few seconds for the news to get there: "Emergency. A bomb in Ben Yehuda."

The ambulances followed a few minutes later.

The fight between Arabs and Jews had heated up since the days of the Hebron massacre. The British, who were in charge of Palestine, had announced their intention to leave. The Jews had announced their intention to create a state of their own, after two thousand years without a homeland and after a Holocaust which had killed six million of their people. The Arabs had announced their plans as well — to kill the Jews and their new state together.

Even before the State of Israel was created, the killing began.

Ben Yehuda was one of Jerusalem's largest and busiest streets. Seven-thirty was one of its busiest times, as Jerusalemites headed toward their offices. When the truck filled with TNT exploded, it caused a huge amount of damage. More than fifty-four people were killed, and over a hundred were injured. Amazingly, this terrible bomb had not been planted by Arabs. It was British soldiers who were behind it.

Shaare Zedek, as the closest large hospital to the disaster, took many of the wounded.

Schvester Selma realized immediately that this was a true emergency. She barked her orders: empty the large room normally used for day patients. Bring in beds, stretchers, blood supplies for transfusions. Call all available doctors and nurses. Get the bandages out. Choose which patients were the most critical and race them to the operating room. Clean up the blood — so much blood! — and examine each new face.

While the head nurse was racing to save lives, her assistant, Margit, was also busy. Hers was a grim task indeed. She was sent down to the basement, where many of the dead had been brought. Together with grieving relatives and confused survivors, she had to try and identify the bodies.

As she stared down at one dark-skinned, dark-haired young woman, Margit's heart seemed to stop. *It can't be,* she thought. *But the WIZO Day Care Center is right next to Ben Yehuda.*

It couldn't be, but it was. Bolissa, Schvester Selma's beloved foster child, had become one of the casualties of the war between the Arabs, the British, and the Jews. The young woman lay dead in the basement of the hospital that had been her home since she'd been a baby.

Schvester Selma had seen many terrible things in her years in Jerusalem. She'd lived through war and famine and epidemics. Though her heart had sometimes broken, she'd always managed to go on and do her job. She'd healed the sick and comforted the bereaved.

Today, though, it was the gallant *schvester* who needed the comfort. Margit broke the terrible news to her. She had expected tears, perhaps screams. There were no tears. There was just a silence almost too awful to bear. Schvester Selma walked quietly to her room. Today, for the first time in more than thirty years, Jerusalem would have to take care of its sick without her.

The next day, tiny Schvester Selma returned to her post. She was quieter, perhaps, than usual. Her step was less springy than it had been the day before. But the dead had to be buried — and the living had to be taken care of. Even in the face of tragedy, Schvester Selma carried on.

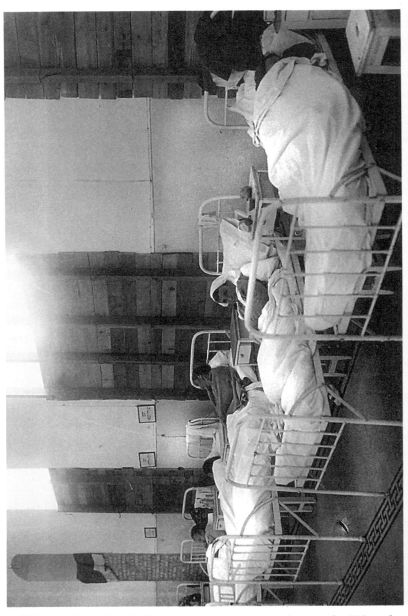

The windows boarded up to protect patients during the War of Independence

Chapter 12

War, Again

Jerusalem, 1947–1948

Every year, without fail, Schvester Selma would take a two-week vacation. She usually spent the time with old friends who lived in Nahariya. Nahariya was a small and pleasant resort town in the north of Israel. It was the perfect place for a tired nurse to get some rest and revive her energy.

It was a few months after her terrible loss. The hospital had been a busy place. There had been more terrorist incidents, more wounded and more dead. Though she wasn't in the mood for fun, Schvester Selma realized she needed to "recharge her batteries." After all, things would certainly get worse before they'd get better. Shaare Zedek needed a head nurse who was rested and who could cope with whatever lay in the future. Selma headed up north.

She was in Nahariya when the incredible news came. The United Nations had voted and agreed — a part of Palestine was to become a Jewish state! Outside, in the city center near the river that cut across the town, young people were dancing excitedly in circles. Schvester Selma, though, didn't join the celebration.

This will surely mean war, she thought to herself. *I must get back to Jerusalem. Now.*

But getting back to Jerusalem — now — wasn't as easy as all that. As soon as the Arabs heard the United Nations vote, their fury erupted. Jerusalem was a city divided between Arab and Jewish neighborhoods. The city now split into two. The streets that bordered Arab and Jewish areas became battlegrounds. No one knew when a bomb would explode. Every building could hide a man with a rifle looking for someone to shoot.

Worst of all, the Arabs cut the city off from the rest of the country. Jerusalem is a city built on hills. There was only one road that connected it to Tel Aviv and the center of Palestine. The Arabs, who lived on the top of the hills, sent bombs and bullets down on any truck or bus foolish enough to try and get to Jerusalem. The trip became a dangerous and deadly one.

When a short little lady with clipped gray hair came to Tel Aviv and announced that she had to get back to Jerusalem, most people laughed, or thought she was mad.

But Schvester Selma wasn't going to let some Arabs on a hill keep her from her beloved hospital. She ran from office to office in Tel Aviv, trying to find a way to re-

ırn. Day followed day, week followed week. The news
ʻom Jerusalem got worse and worse. The Arabs had cut
ff the only water pipeline to the Jewish neighborhoods.
Jow the Jews had only the water they had saved in cis-
ɛrns, deep stone-lined rooms made to store rainwater.
ood was getting harder to find, since trucks couldn't
ɛt through.

Schvester Selma knew her people needed her. She
ʻied the British, but they weren't interested in helping
ɛws. All they cared about was getting out of Palestine and
ɔing back home. She tried the new government that was
ɛing formed, but everyone was too busy to help her. She
ʻied the underground army that was hoping to defend
ɪe new state, but again, there was no one to talk to.

One of Schvester Selma's beliefs was that if you try
ard enough, things work out. After three weeks of
ork, she was awakened in her hotel room by a knock at
ɪe door. A young man wearing a shabby army uniform
ood before her. "Get your things now, Schvester. We're
ɛnding a convoy to Jerusalem, and you've been cleared
ɔ join it."

The only way to get to Jerusalem was through these
ɔnvoys. They were long lines of buses and trucks that
ould drive together through the night. Their lights were
ɛpt off so the Arabs on the top of the hills shouldn't see
ɪem. Their windows were covered with metal to help
ɔrotect them from bullets.

It was a wild and frightening ride. The convoy chose
moonless night so they could stay better hidden.

A convoy snakes its way up to Jerusalem

Slowly, ever so slowly, they ground up the steep hill
The drivers leaned forward, desperately trying to see th
road before them in the deep blackness. The rule was,
one truck or bus was hit, or ran off the road, you left hi
behind. The goal: Jerusalem. With food, with bandage
with medicine, and with army supplies and soldiers de
perately needed in the besieged city. And, this time, wit
one civilian: Schvester Selma.

Today the ride from Tel Aviv to Jerusalem takes
comfortable forty-five minutes. When Schvester Seln
came back to her home, it took most of the night. Inc
by inch they climbed. Once, a few bullets made
rat-tat-tat on the armored side of her bus. Schvestı
Selma readied herself to treat anyone hit, but luckily tl
bullets didn't get through the metal walls. The convo
moved on, ignoring the bullets.

Somehow, some way, this convoy got through. chvester Selma had never thought the stone walls of haare Zedek could look so beautiful as they did that ay, glowing pink in the early morning Jerusalem sun.

She was home.

There wasn't much time to rejoice in her return. haare Zedek was busier than ever. Jerusalem's other rge hospital, Hadassah, on the top of Mount Scopus, as surrounded by Arabs. Though it remained in Jewish ands, it was cut off and could no longer take in pa- ents. All the many wounded, plus the usual sick peo- e, turned up at Schvester Selma's doorstep.

The city was slowly starving. Luckily, Shaare Zedek d many of its own supplies. Dr. Wallach had insisted keeping his own cows, to ensure the kashruth of the ilk. Now, in besieged Jerusalem, only patients in 'allach's Hospital had the luxury of hot cereal cooled wn with a bit of milk. Much of the city sat in dark- ss, as electric lines were cut. But the lights of Shaare edek, with its own generator for Shabbat use, shone d twinkled. The food situation was difficult. Many eals were just black bread that tasted like cardboard, neared with oil to make it softer. If you were lucky, you so got a piece of salty lakerda fish. Old Jerusalemite omen knew which weeds could be boiled into a tasty up. The seeds of sunflowers, when baked, made a fill- g snack.

If food was scarce, water was as precious as dia- onds. The faucets, when opened, dripped tiny drops.

Every city resident was allowed a small amount of wat
per day, just enough to live on.

Things were bad when the United Nations voted
create a state for the Jews. Things got much worse whe
the State of Israel was actually declared. Enough of te
rorist attacks. This was all out war! The armies of mar
Arab countries descended upon the new state and, pa
ticularly, on its capital, Jerusalem. There were terribl
bloody battles.

One day, Dr. Wallach called the nurses and docto
together. "The soldiers have told me they expect the ci
to be shelled. Our hospital is built well. If a bomb hits,
will probably not break through the walls. Stay out
the hallways. They are not built as well, and if a shell hi
there, it can cause terrible damage."

The army was right this time. The shells began fa
ing throughout the city. There would be a whistle,
whoosh, and then an awful *boom!* Anyone nearby wou
fall to the ground, hoping not to be hit.

Shaare Zedek had always been a hospital whe
Shabbat had been carefully kept. It is said, "More tha
the Jewish people have kept Shabbat, Shabbat has ke
the Jewish people." Perhaps Dr. Wallach's loving care
the laws of Shabbat was what protected his hospital or
hot Shabbat morning.

Margit, Schvester Selma's assistant, was just prepa
ing to put an intravenous tube into the arm of a frigh
ened little boy. She was in a large room next to the buil
ing's main hallway. Suddenly, she heard it: the awful, i

scapable whistle of an oncoming shell. To her horror, she saw the large, bullet-shaped object come flying straight toward the hallway. She could heard Dr. Wallach's voice: "Stay out of the hallways...they are not built as well...terrible damage..."

With a *whoosh* and a *whump* the shell landed right in the middle of the hallway. It raised a cloud of dust that covered everything, including the frightened little boy. Margit held her breath and waited for the explosion.

It never came. The shell landed, unexploded, right in the stairs. There it lay, in a pile of dust, like a giant dead whale washed up on a beach.

The saddest day of the entire war happened not long afterwards. The Old City of Jerusalem, surrounded by a wall, had been besieged by Arabs for many weeks. There was no food. There was no water. And, finally, there was no hope. While the Jews were winning many battles throughout the land, they lost the battle for the Old City.

Over a thousand women, children, and old men gathered together in a famous old shul, the Eliyahu HaNavi Synagogue. Some were wounded. Many were dying. Their husbands and sons and fathers had been taken prisoner by the Arabs. These people were going to be let go. They were homeless now.

On the night the Old City fell, there were many wounded. The shriek of ambulances split the darkness. Miriam, now a young nurse, spent the entire evening taking care of the patients. Some were put into the dining room. Others spent the time moaning in the hall ways.

Miriam finally returned, exhausted, to her tiny room in the basement of the hospital. She found an entire family camped out on her bed.

Yosef, the man who ran the laundry, quickly explained. "They are my wife and children. We live — we lived — in the Old City. We have no home."

"But this is my room," Miriam whispered.

"I've spoken to Dr. Wallach. He said we could stay here. Please," the man said, giving her a pleading look, "my babies have no place to go."

I have no place of my own in the entire world, Miriam thought to herself. Looking at the little ones on her bed, she sighed. They, too, had no place.

Miriam peered out into the darkness. She listened, but there was no sound of shells. Quickly, she raced toward a small building the nursing school sometimes used. The door was locked, but a window was open.

The next morning, Schvester Selma walked into her office in the nursing school building. She stopped at the sight of a woman sleeping soundly on her desk. Then she tiptoed closer.

With a smile and a sigh, Schvester Selma found a blanket and covered the exhausted nurse.

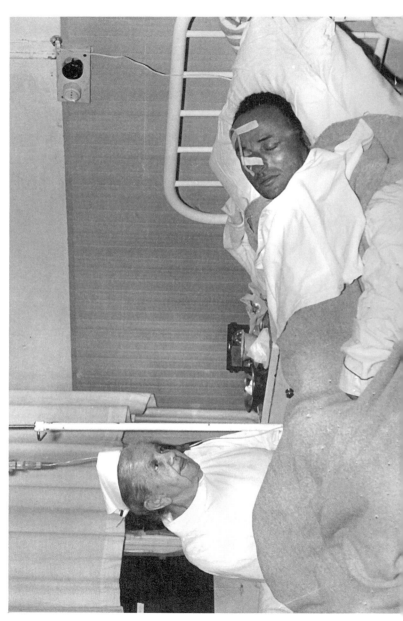

Schvester Selma, caring for wounded soldiers;
1917, 1948 and here in 1967

Chapter 13

Endings and Beginnings

Jerusalem, 1948–1984

Time is a strange thing. When a person gets older, time seems to go faster. So it was that the years after Israel became a state just flew by.

In the walls of Shaare Zedek Hospital, people were born. People died. People grew ill. People were healed. Whatever happened, there were two people close by to help: Dr. Wallach and Schvester Selma.

Dr. Wallach worked full-time until he was eighty years old. Even at eighty-five, he would spend an entire night at the bedside of a patient very ill with pneumonia.

And Schvester Selma? She, like her mentor, her boss, and her friend, worked until she was very old. At seventy-five, Schvester Selma was still teaching her nurses. If she saw a piece of dust on the floor, she would still bend down to pick it up.

But even the great grow old. In her nineties, Schvester Selma spent most of her time sitting on the hospital grounds, remembering. Her adopted daughter, Samoocha, faithfully tended to her needs.

Sometimes Selma would stare at her finger, at the very unexpected object that twinkled upon it.

A woman had appeared one day a few years earlier. She requested an interview with Schvester Selma.

"Yes? Can I help you?" Selma asked.

"My sister was deported and killed by the Nazis. We lived in Vienna."

Schvester Selma's wrinkled face showed her sympathy. "I am sorry."

"My sister knew she would never come back from the death camps. Before she left, she gave me this."

The woman pulled a small box out of her pocketbook. She opened it. Inside was a beautiful, sparkling diamond ring.

"Before she was deported, she told me I was to give this ring away."

"Away?"

"Yes. If she did not return — and she knew she would not — I was to find a woman who had never married. A woman who had given her whole life for others. I was to give her the ring."

The woman looked seriously at Schvester Selma. "I have read of your life, of what you've done. This ring belongs to you."

Now, resting in the courtyard, Selma would stare at

Mayor Teddy Kollek presents award of "Jerusalem Notable" to Schvester Selma

the brilliant diamond. It sparkled in the strong Jerusalem sunshine. She would stare at it and remember.

She remembered a young girl in the Heine Hospital making a decision to come to a strange new land. She remembered the mud that had eaten her boots so often. The odd, eccentric, and wonderfully kind man who screamed so loud and yet laughed so often. The sweet little babies she'd cared for and poor Bolissa whose life was cut short. She remembered wars and blood and peace and serenity.

Once, a long, long time ago, young Schvester Selma

had sat on a train winding its way up through the mountains of Turkey. Selma could remember the thin ribbon of track going up, up, up. *Perhaps it is reaching all the way to heaven*, she had thought then with a laugh.

Now, looking at this hospital that she loved, at this city that had grown so much, she wondered if she hadn't been right after all.

All the way to heaven, she thought.

Glossary

Aliyah: Immigration to Israel.

Aron kodesh: Literally, "holy ark"; where Torah scrolls are kept in synagogue.

Baruch Hashem: Thank God.

Bris: Circumcision.

Chalav Yisrael: Milk under Jewish supervision from the time of milking.

Chanukah: Festival of Lights.

Havdalah: Ceremony marking the end of Shabbat.

Ima: Mother.

Kashruth: The dietary laws.

Kever: Tomb.

Mezuzah: Parchment inscribed with Shema, rolled and put into a case which is attached to the doorpost.

Mohel: One who performs circumcision.

Shul: Synagogue.

Tehillim: Psalms.

Yarmulke: Skullcap.